THE PUN

FOLLY *fol'i, n* silliness or weakness of mind; a foolish thing; a monument of folly, such as one left unfinished because it was begun without establishing the cost.

PUNDIT *pun'dit, n* a learned man; an authority, now, commonly, someone who considers himself or herself an authority.

Chambers Concise Dictionary,
Edinburgh, 1991

THE PUNDIT'S FOLLY

Chronicles of an Empty Life

Sinclair B. Ferguson

THE BANNER OF TRUTH TRUST

THE BANNER OF TRUTH TRUST
3 Murrayfield Road, Edinburgh EH12 6EL
P.O. Box 621, Carlisle, Pennsylvania 17013, USA

*

First Published 1995
Reprinted 2000
ISBN 0 85151 676 9

*

Typeset in 11/12pt Erhardt MT
and 12/13pt Biffo MT
Printed and bound in Great Britain by
Caledonian International Book Manufacturing Ltd, Glasgow

*

To

Bill and Jean Wallace

Wise and Faithful Friends

The world is a sea of glass: a pageant of fond delight,
a theatre of vanity, a labyrinth of error,
a gulf of grief, a sty of filthiness, a vale of misery,
a spectacle of woe, a river of tears, a stage of deceit,
a cage full of devils, a den of scorpions,
a wilderness of wolves, a cabin of bears,
a whirlwind of passions, a fained comedy,
a delectable frenzy; where is false delight, assured
grief; certain sorrow, uncertain pleasure; lasting woe,
fickle wealth; long heaviness,
short joy.

—Arthur Dent,
The Plain Man's Pathway to Heaven

CONTENTS

1: Chasing the Wind

In chase of fancied happiness, still woo'd
And never won. Dream after dream ensues;
And still they dream that they shall still succeed,
And still are disappointed.

WILLIAM COWPER

1

Outside of the town of Oban, on the west coast of Scotland, stands a remarkable building. It overlooks the bay and, viewed from a distance, rises Colosseum-like in its grandeur; floodlit at night, its appearance is as unusual as it is unexpected.

But the sightseers who make their way to it in the full light of day must prepare themselves for disappointment. The building, many-windowed and wonderfully symmetrical, is a mere shell. There is no glazing in the windows; there is no inside; it is, and always has been, simply a circular wall. Its only practical value has been that it once gave building workers employment in the off-season. This edifice, now a century old, is named after its builder, McCaig's *Folly*.

The word 'folly' is derived from the French *folie*, 'foolishness'. Many such buildings litter the British countryside; others can be found in France. Most of them date from the eighteenth and early nineteenth centuries. These varied constructions are usually impressively and expensively built in the classical or Gothic style. They have one thing in common: they were constructed to impress but they serve no real function; they are useless and empty. Follies they are and foolish were their wealthy builders.

Throughout the ages men and women, great and small, rich and poor, well-known and unknown have built such follies. Sometimes, as in the case of McCaig, they have been physical constructions; always they have been attempts of one individual or another to give his or her life significance. The implication is that there must be more to life than the mere living of it.

But, without exception, these monuments to the achievements of an individual meet the fate Shelley describes in his poem *Ozymandias*:

> I met a traveller from an antique land,
> Who said – 'Two vast and trunkless legs of stone
> Stand in the desert . . . Near them, on the sand,
> Half sunk a shattered visage lies, whose frown,
> And wrinkled lip, and sneer of cold command,
> Tell that its sculptor well those passions read
> Which yet survive, stamped on these lifeless things,
> The hand that mocked them, and the heart that fed;
> And on the pedestal, these words appear:
> My name is Ozymandias, King of Kings,
> Look on my Works, ye Mighty, and despair!
> Nothing beside remains. Round the decay
> Of that colossal wreck, boundless and bare
> The lone and level sands stretch far away.'

But surely there is meaning to life? A Leonardo da Vinci, a Michelangelo, a Shakespeare, a Dostoevsky – surely these are lives with significance? Perhaps. Yet what were these men's great works but expressions of their hungry quest to give significance to lives they otherwise feared had none? The result? To us their lives have significance; but no longer for themselves. Rich and poor, the talented and the ordinary – we come to the same end. Some of the things we have done last; but of each of us the endlessly repeated words will be intoned: 'earth to earth' or 'ashes to ashes'. We cannot take with us the monuments we seek to build to our own significance. Death, as they say, is the Great Leveller.

Can there be any real and lasting purpose if dust is our destiny? Is life meaningful, or meaningless?

The question has a modern ring about it. But it is really an ancient one. In fact some of the most penetrating reflections on it are found in an ancient near-eastern book called 'Ecclesiastes', or in the language in which it was originally written, *Qoheleth*.

Who and what was this *Qoheleth*? The name is really a title. It means the Public Teacher. Perhaps we might call him 'the Professor', or even better, 'the Pundit' the learned man, or at least the person who believes he can speak as an authority.

Here is how his book begins:

> *Meaningless! Meaningless! . . .*
> *Utterly meaningless!*
> *Everything is meaningless.*[1]

The same sentiment is still in his mind as he comes near to its end:

> *Meaningless! Meaningless! . . .*
> *Everything is meaningless!*[2]

In fact he uses the word 'meaningless' no less than thirty-five times in the course of his chronicles.

Here, then, is a tale of searching, of experimenting, of groping for meaning. Nor was this done in an ivory tower, although the Pundit certainly had academic qualifications. But he did not confine his experiments to the laboratory or his researches to the library. He pursued his education in the 'university of life'.

The Pundit was a talented man, gifted with a well-developed critical faculty. He could analyse things clearly and wrote in a pungent style.

[1] Ecclesiastes 1:2 [2] Eccl. 12:8

Admittedly his experiences seem larger-than-life by comparison with ours; and he was also able to describe them more vividly than most of us can. Perhaps he had a more enquiring mind than many, and was more energetic in his quest for meaning than we tend to be. In his day the issues of life may have been more obvious than they are in ours. Our society may be more short-sighted than his, or perhaps just more insensitive.

There, however, the differences between the Pundit and ourselves end. In most other respects our lives and his are mirror images.

But the Pundit made a discovery, one that is shared by many of our contemporaries: he found it difficult to trace any satisfying meaning running through his life. Despite his best efforts to avoid the conclusion, he began to wonder whether his life was bankrupt of any significance lasting beyond the moment. He could find no explanation of things which made sense of the world and his own place in it.

That was not due to any lack of effort on his part. Early in his journey in search of meaning, he came to a crossroads. Faced with the challenge of trying to make sense of life he realised that there were several routes he might try: one was education; another was pleasure; then there was work; finally came the prospect of success. Surely in one of them he would find what he was looking for?

In fact, he was so earnest in his quest that he explored each of the roads in turn. He tells us what happened.

EDUCATION

The Pundit chose the intellectual path first of all. In a way, that was the natural thing for him to do, because he possessed considerable intellectual ability. But he was not interested in merely keeping his brain ticking over. He really thought that the answer to his deep-seated unrest might be found in education: surely the wisdom of the ages and the wonders of science hold the key to life?

> *I devoted myself to study and to explore*
> *by wisdom all that is done under heaven.*[1]

His assumption was this: ignorance is our greatest enemy; if only we can increase in knowledge and understanding we will begin to solve more of the problems that curse our lives and our world and make so much of it seem meaningless.

To his credit, the Pundit was involved in instructing the young; but he also had an acute concern for society in general. He saw the needs: young people in his day, as in ours, needed an adequate education. Without it their lives would be empty and aimless. No wonder, then, if there is so much poverty, prejudice and crime. You can almost hear him say: 'What is needed in these areas, of course, is more education; the Government must increase its commitment *in real terms.*' More education is what we need. It is the only guarantee of a better society.

We do need better education. Good education, for ourselves and for our children, ought always to be high on our list of priorities. But to think that more and better education is the answer to the quest for meaning is one of the most serious mistakes we can make.

Why? Because information in the mind cannot of itself satisfy the needs of the heart. Nor can it tame the unruliness of the soul.

The western world has had more widespread educational opportunities than any civilisation in human history. Are we more deeply satisfied and well-ordered as individuals or societies as a result? More technologically advanced, yes; but *better* or *happier*? Is the hunger for meaning satisfied?

[1] Eccl. 1:13

To ask the question is to answer it. Read the newspapers; the answer is written large on every front page. Watch television; the answer is found in every news bulletin.

We have a more highly educated society than ever; but we also have more expressions of greed, more crime, more violence, and correspondingly more fear.

We have more education about racism; but do we really have any less racial discrimination arising in the heart?

We have more sex-education. Politicians and educationalists introduced it partly because they were alarmed at the number of illegitimate births. Result? It is doubtful if fewer babies are conceived; rather, there are only less live births. It is not sex education that has kept down the illegitimacy rate, but abortion. A new term has recently had to be coined: 'date-rape'. The disconcerting thing about it is that it belongs to the world of our most highly educated young people.

Where will you find the most offensive graffiti? In the massive and socially under-provided housing projects where the educational standards are low? Perhaps. But in all likelihood no graffiti surpasses the vulgarity of that found in abundance on some of the walls of our universities. Here some of our brightest minds give expression to their cynical, ill-disciplined and sometimes spiteful souls. Education may have filled the mind, but in itself it has no power to cleanse or to tame the spirit.

In what context do you find the most shameful breaches of decency in relation to members of the opposite sex? Among the lowest-educated members of society? No. Today we find them in reports of parties held among highly-educated military personnel. Here are young men who have received an expensive, extensive, highly-demanding education for their minds; yet their behaviour expresses the continuing distortions of the most educated human heart.

No, the idea that education as such can solve our real

problems whether personal or communal is a myth long-exploded by the harsh realities of life. This, at least, was a conclusion the Pundit quickly reached:

> *I have seen all the things that are done under*
> *the sun; all of them are meaningless,*
> *a chasing after the wind.*[1]

The pursuit of education appeared to be the answer to his needs; until he found that education in itself merely informs. It has no power of its own to purify:

> *What is twisted cannot be straightened;*
> *what is lacking cannot be counted.*[2]

The greatest benefit of a good education has always been that it enables us to think clearly. We learn to draw different kinds of logically straight lines and how to count in a variety of ways – in highly sophisticated forms and modes. But, says the Pundit, there are some things that education, even the best education, is powerless to do: it cannot untangle the twists in the human heart; it cannot make up for what is lacking in the soul. Perhaps he too had noticed that some of the most intelligent and well-educated individuals are among the saddest and most tortured of people.

Now, of course this may be true, we may think, if our interest in education is concentrated on the hard sciences (counting and untwisting, to use the Pundit's imagery!). What is really needed is a broader education which gives us exposure to the treasures of our literary, musical and aesthetic inheritance. There is so much we can learn from the history of the nations. The riches of the wisdom of the ages are available to us. Surely a 'classical' education would give us the answers we seek?

[1] Eccl. 1:14 [2] Eccl. 1:15

But the Pundit knew all about that. Yes, he agreed: 'wisdom is better than folly'.[1] But he had pursued this avenue as well, fruitlessly:

I thought to myself, 'Look, I have
grown and increased in wisdom more than
anyone who has ruled . . . before me;
I have experienced much of wisdom and
knowledge.' Then I applied myself to the
understanding of wisdom, and also of madness
and folly, but I learned that this, too, is a
chasing after the wind.
For with much wisdom comes much sorrow;
the more knowledge, the more grief.[2]

G. F. Hegel's well-known lament that 'All we learn from history is that we learn nothing from history' is only a half-truth. Nevertheless the whole truth is that the lessons of the past cannot satisfy the needs of the human heart today. The Pundit recognised that 'wisdom is better than folly'. But whether we pursue wisdom or exhibit folly, are wise men or fools, the net result of our lives appears to be the same:

The same fate overtakes them both.[3]

At the end of the day there is an emptiness in human learning and wisdom: it is emptiness and meaninglessness. It is not an end in itself; seeking meaning for our lives by pursuing education on its own is like chasing the wind.

I have never forgotten an experience I had as a student. My philosophy of religion tutor had asked me to come to see him to discuss a paper I had written. I was a young Christian

[1] Eccl. 2:13 [2] Eccl. 1:16–18 [3] Eccl. 2:14

believer; he made no Christian commitment and his lectures consistently sought to undermine the coherence of the Christian faith.

To my pleasure (and surprise!) he had given my paper a good grade. But there my encouragement ended. We talked about what I had written for well over an hour. I was amazed he was willing to spend so much time discussing – the first two sentences of the paper! We could not get beyond them. We were unable to agree on the starting point for clear thinking about either God or man. As the Pundit would have said, what is twisted cannot be straightened, and what is lacking cannot be counted!

Many students, I knew, took at least one course in philosophy because they thought it might help them to answer the deepest questions in life. For my part, I left my tutor's room feeling that anyone who thought that education would reward their quest for meaning and certainty would be chasing after the wind. Sharpen the intellect it might, but satisfy the quest for meaning it never can.

The Pundit may have had a similar experience. Education, he discovered, is vital; but it cannot meet the deepest longings of the heart. It can never teach us the meaning of life. That realisation seems to have brought him back to the crossroads to try one of the other paths along which meaning and satisfaction might be found.

PLEASURE

He became a pleasure-seeker, or, to use the more sophisticated terminology, he tried the pathway of 'Hedonism':

> *I thought in my heart, 'Come now, I will*
> *test you with pleasure to find out what is good.'*[1]

[1] Eccl. 2:1

He continues,

> *I denied myself nothing my eyes desired;*
> *I refused my heart no pleasure.*[1]

Imagine it! Anything that you see and want, anything that your heart desires, and you can have it! What would you choose? 'Here is satisfaction at last,' you might think.

A hauntingly contemporary spirit had surely gripped the Pundit at this point: what mattered now to him, indeed all that mattered, was to have 'a good time'.

What does that mean today? Laughter, sex, and drink come most immediately to mind.

The Pundit himself pursued this hedonistic path. He seems to have become the consummate late twentieth century good-time-haver. Here is what he did:

A Good Laugh

Laughter is the sign we are having a good time and enjoying ourselves. Sometimes there is truth in that, although we should never confuse 'having a good laugh' with 'having a sense of humour'. Some of those with the most sharply-honed sense of humour do not actually laugh a great deal!

Laughter can do us great good. It can do us emotional good because it usually means we have learned to see things from an unexpected point of view. Laughing at ourselves can be a very healthy thing; laughing at something or even at someone else (so long as they share the pleasures of the laughter) can be an expression of shared love and affection.

Yet this is by no means the whole truth. And sometimes it is not even the partial truth. The pleasures of laughter can also be the gratification of cruelty, even an expression of hatred or jealousy.

But most of the time the truth is that laughter is simply empty. Watch even a 'clean' comedy on television or on

[1] Eccl. 2:10

the stage; compare the after-effect with that of watching a tragedy. From the very beginnings of drama the difference has been well-recognised. Comedy is light, tragedy is weighty; comedy is superficial; but a good tragedy is able to produce a *catharsis* of the emotions, like a medicine that cleanses pollutants out of the system and makes it function properly again.

That was certainly the experience of the Pundit. He thought that he could have a good time by having a good laugh. But listen to what he discovered:

> *'Laughter,' I said, 'is foolish'.*[1]
> *Sorrow is better than laughter,*
> *because a sad face is good for the heart . . .*
> *Like the crackling of thorns under the pot,*
> *so is the laughter of fools.*
> *This too is meaningless.*[2]

Why? Why is 'a good cry' often better for us than 'a good laugh'? Perhaps because life is no laughing matter; or because we see some things more clearly when our vision has been cleansed by tears.

Is all there is to life the obsession with having a good laugh? The Pundit realised that if ever that became true of him he must surely be one of the saddest men on earth.

I do not know whether the famous author G. K. Chesterton laughed a great deal, but he certainly had a remarkable sense of humour. He was a very solidly built person. One day as he walked down a London street, clad in his famous cape-like cloak, he turned a corner and was immediately knocked over by someone coming in the opposite direction who was carrying a grandfather clock! Chesterton was spread-eagled on the ground, but as he looked up and realised what had happened, his sense of the

[1] Eccl. 2:2 [2] Eccl. 7:3, 6.

ridiculous and his love of humour took over: 'Why can't you wear a wrist-watch like everyone else?' he demanded!

But the same humour-loving Chesterton made the striking observation that we have no record of Jesus of Nazareth ever laughing. Perhaps he did; presumably he did. But the point is that laughter was not such a predominant feature of his life that any of the Gospel writers felt that it was important to mention it: pity, compassion, love, tears, pain – yes; but not laughter.

Yet who can read the Gospels and fail to realise that here, at last, with Jesus of Nazareth, we discover the satisfied man? No, 'a good laugh' is not the prescription for lasting joy.

A Good Drink

Here is how the Pundit puts it:

> *I tried cheering myself with wine.*[1]

'Nothing wrong with a good wine' we might well respond. Why even the Bible speaks about the 'wine that gladdens the heart of man' being a gift from God (Psalm 104:15). What is wrong with good wine, then?

The Pundit has no interest in the merits or demerits of abstinence from alcohol. He is not despising those who drink wine as though to do so were ungodly. What he is talking about is drinking wine to try to lift himself out of his depressing emptiness. Wine had become more to him than one of the good things in life; it was now a drug to mask the unsatisfied longings of his soul. He had hoped it would act as a stimulant, and had discovered instead that it was a further depressant.

There is a great gulf between drinking wine to enjoy the taste, and drinking it in order to dull the conscience. The Pundit wanted to dull his senses and to find respite from his deepest heartaches. It was almost as though he could hear

[1] Eccl. 2:3

reverberating in his mind the too-well remembered dissatisfactions of yesterday and the emptiness of tomorrow:

Ah, fill the Cup: – what boots it to repeat
How time is slipping underneath our Feet:
  Unborn TO-MORROW and dead YESTERDAY,
Why fret about them if TO-DAY be sweet![1]

The words of the famous Rolling Stones' song could not have been more appropriate to the Pundit's feelings: 'I can't get no satisfaction'. He gazed into his wine glass in the vain hope that there he might find the switch which would turn off the record and give him peace. But all he saw was the reflection of his own emptiness.

We call it 'pleasure-seeking' but the truth is we should really call it 'escapism'. It exists in a dozen guises, only one of which is alcoholic. The reality from which we take flight also exists in many forms: we flee from our own failure, from a marriage or relationship gone sour, from the past, from the future, from the present, from our inability to exercise self-control – or from a hundred other dissatisfactions.

The excitement of 'an affair' – strange euphemism – at whatever level, may seem to help us forget the failures in our marriage; other disappointments may be compensated for by over-drinking, over-eating, even over-exposure to TV soaps. Whatever we substitute for facing up to reality, we learn the hard way that flight is not the answer. It leaves us with the same gnawing emptiness with which we started.

That was the Pundit's testimony. He was by no means alone; it is all too common a lament:

I tried the broken cisterns Lord,
But ah! the waters failed,
Ev'n as I stooped to drink they fled
  And mocked me as I wailed.[2]

[1] Edward Fitzgerald, *Rubaiyat of Omar Khayyam of Naishapur*, xxxvii
[2] Anonymous, from 'O Christ in thee my soul hath found'

A Good Time

He was in a position most of us would envy. He could afford a good time! There were no financial restrictions to make him think, 'If only I could . . . '. If only we could resolve the great 'if only' in our lives how different they would be!

But here was someone who was able to do virtually anything that he wanted to do:

> *I built houses [note the plural!] for myself and planted vineyards. I made gardens and parks and planted all kinds of fruit trees in them. I made reservoirs to water groves of flourishing trees . . .*
> *I . . . owned more herds and flocks than anyone . . .*
> *I amassed silver and gold for myself . . . men and women singers, and a harem as well – the delights of the heart of man.*[1]

What can you say, except 'Wow!'? Imagine being able to say, 'I denied myself nothing my heart desired' and to be simply speaking the truth!

Possessions, power, influence, beautiful things enjoyed in beautiful surroundings and with beautiful people – all were his for the asking or the taking.

Be honest. Isn't this the kind of lifestyle you secretly hanker after? When people are asked what they think heaven is like, their picture of it is usually a fair approximation of the Pundit's lifestyle; heaven is having whatever you want. He had heaven on earth!

Or did he? Listen again to him:

> *Yet when I surveyed all that my hands had done*
> *and what I had toiled to achieve,*
> *everything was meaningless, a chasing*
> *after the wind;*
> *nothing was gained under the sun.*[2]

[1] Eccl. 2:4–9 [2] Eccl. 2:11

How many people do you know who have found lasting satisfaction in having a good time? None. To seek it in the good-time life is to chase after the wind. It is an endless pursuit of what we can never attain. Our desires are never satisfied; we go from one well to another seeking water to quench our thirst. But the wells of the pleasure-seekers are empty.

This explains why the pleasure-*seekers* can never be pleasure-*keepers*.

Robert Burns the Scottish poet knew this and described it as eloquently as human pen has ever done:

> But pleasures are like poppies spread
> You seize the flower, the bloom is shed
> Or like the snow falls in the river
> A moment white, then melts for ever . . .
> Or like the rainbow's lovely form
> Evanishing amid the storm.[1]

Why is this? Because these pleasures cannot last. And, as the Pundit himself discovered, even if they did, our ability to be satisfied with pleasures does not last:

> *Remember your Creator in the days of your*
> *youth,*
> *before the days of trouble come*
> *and the years approach when you will say,*
> *'I find no pleasure in them'.*[2]

The way of the hedonist fails. The tragedy is this: since we do not find lasting pleasures, and do not discover lasting satisfaction in them, our ability to find any satisfaction begins to disappear. The satisfaction addict is no more able to say 'I have had enough, I am satisfied' than is the drug addict. There is never enough in this world to satisfy us.

[1] *Tam o' Shanter*, 59 [2] Eccl. 12:1

At the end the sad complaint of the elderly becomes ours too, 'I have few pleasures left'. That is often an exaggeration – but not because there are endless pleasures left. Rather, it is usually a way of saying, 'I have *no* real pleasures. But since I have lived for pleasures all my life, I cannot face the terrible truth that there are none left to taste; or if there are, I find I can no longer taste them.' How desperately sad; how tragically true.

WORK

If neither education nor the quest for pleasure could bring the Pundit a sense of purpose and fulfilment, what other roads could he take? Returning to the crossroads he threw himself into work and business.

So the Pundit became a workaholic. There was hard toil. He poured all his efforts and skill into his achievements. Nor were these inconsiderable.

And yet he became deeply disillusioned once more. Worse still, he found himself a *bitterly* disappointed man:

> *I hated life, because the work that is done under the sun was grievous to me. All of it is meaningless, a chasing after the wind. I hated all the things I had toiled for under the sun, because I must leave them to the one who comes after me . . . my heart began to despair over all my toilsome labour . . .*
> *What does a man get for all the toil and anxious striving with which he labours . . . All his days his work is pain and grief; even at night his mind does not rest . . .*[1]

It is hard to believe this was written three thousand years ago. It sounds all too like the random thoughts of a modern

[1] Eccl. 2:17-23

businessman during a session with his psychotherapist. Look at the vocabulary which dominates the description of his work: 'meaningless', 'chasing', 'hated', 'toiled', 'despair', 'anxious striving', 'pain and grief'! What has happened?

He had made an idol of his work; it filled his horizon. But then he discovered it could not deliver the satisfaction the situations vacant advertisement promised him.

In every area of life it is the same. When we discover that our idols have feet of clay our distaste for them is usually in direct proportion to our earlier devotion to them; it tends to be as wholehearted as was the pursuit and the short-lived pleasure. Now the Pundit saw things in a different and clearer light, and what he saw left him feeling he had been deceived in his pursuit of satisfaction.

Why?

For one thing he realised that he was building castles in the air; all his work was insecure. He saw now that there was nothing he could do to guarantee its permanence. The day would come when the reins of power would slip out of his hands and be taken over by another. It might be a son or daughter he loved; but even so, in a few years there would be nothing he could do to guarantee the future security of the business. His son or daughter might have no interest in it; or worse, a relative might destroy it. The time would come when he would be powerless to do anything even if his most hated business rival attempted to buy the company. All his labour was really just chasing after the wind.

The first and still the most poignant example of this occurs in the opening chapters of the Book of Genesis.

There Adam is portrayed by calling and profession as a market gardener and the keeper of an extensive private zoo. He enjoyed enormous resources on both sides of these interests! The task to which he devoted himself was the tilling of the soil, the subduing of the earth, and the tending of the animal kingdom for the glory of the Creator.

But what became of him? He committed idolatry. Along with Eve he could not resist the temptation 'Eat from the tree of the knowledge of good and evil and you shall be like God himself'.[1] He grasped for independence by making himself the centre of the universe; he sought satisfaction in the fruit of the garden and the relationships of this world. Instead he found himself under a curse. His work became frustrating and hard, rather than fruitful and enjoyable. The final enigma was that he was told that, eventually, he would disintegrate into the raw materials of his own labour and become dust: 'dust you are and to dust you will return'.[2] Adam who looked after the animals was eventually trodden upon by the very beasts he nurtured![3]

The Pundit also experienced this bitter frustration and disappointment. Instead of finding security in the expansion of his business and the financial success which followed, he experienced more and more anxiety and insomnia: 'the abundance of a rich man permits him no sleep', he wrote.[4] Instead of being satisfied with what he had accomplished he felt he must always be expanding in order to try to secure what had already been achieved. He was in an ever-tightening downward spiral of tension and anxiety. And in the end he realised it was not worth it.

Here is his message: those who seek their ultimate satisfaction and the basic meaning of their lives in work discover only one thing: it is a jungle out there, a dog-eat-dog world. One day you are devouring the competitor, the next you are being devoured. If we behave like animals we end up sharing their final destiny:

> *As for men, God tests them so that they may see that they are like the animals. Man's fate is like*

[1] Genesis 3:5 [2] Gen. 3:19 [3] See Gen. 2:19–20; 3:19 [4] Eccl. 5:12

that of the animals; the same fate awaits them both . . . Everything is meaningless. All go to the same place . . .[1]

Man is not a naked ape, as the secular humanist claims. Sadly, however, his behaviour is often less dignified than that of the animal world. At last the Pundit saw into his own heart:

I saw that all labour and all achievement spring from man's envy of his neighbour. This too is meaningless, a chasing after the wind.[2]

As we shall see, there is another side to work, a new perspective on it, and thankfully the Pundit later discovered it. Eventually he would learn the lasting enjoyment that can be found in it, even in the face of life's uncertainties. But that would come about only when he had learned a salutary lesson:

Better one handful with tranquillity than two handfuls with toil and chasing after the wind.[3]

There was one further route open to him. It seems that the Pundit himself did not take it; he had had enough. But while he was devoting himself to his business he frequently saw others who were on this track. Its terrain was very familiar to him by that time; in fact for much of the way it ran along the same route: success at any price.

SUCCESS

The Pundit observed those who were, in the modern jargon, 'upwardly mobile'. In his society – as in some still today – such people climbed their way up the ladder within the state system. But whether in a capitalist or a socialist society

[1] Eccl. 3:18–20 [2] Eccl. 4:4 [3] Eccl. 4:6

the principle is always the same: job titles, perks, advancement and promotion begin to dominate the horizon. The Pundit, now a chastened and wiser individual, reflected on what happens:

> *If you see the poor oppressed in a district, and justice and rights denied, do not be surprised at such things; for one official is eyed by a higher one, and over them both are others higher still. The increase from the land is taken by all; the king himself profits from the fields.*[1]

The rich get more, the poor get less; financial differentials widen all the time; trust breaks down, suspicion is bred; satisfaction is sought on the next rung of the ladder, in the executive title, in the high specification car. 'Happiness is a status symbol' is the epigram of such a lifestyle.

But what does this kind of upward mobility cost? At the end of the day we find that we have spent all our spiritual resources on financing the journey upwards; on arrival we have sold everything of lasting value.

The Pundit spells out four lessons:

Money does not bring satisfaction with it. Often, and for a variety of reasons, it creates new sorrows and brings people into a new bondage. There must always be a hunger for more:

> *Whoever loves money never has money enough; whoever loves wealth is never satisfied with his income.*[2]

Possessions never bring security to those who trust them for it. The greater the possessions the greater the need for

[1] Eccl. 5:8–9 [2] Eccl. 5:10

insurance! 'What benefit are they to the owner' asks the Pundit, 'except to feast his eyes on them?' Possessions cannot talk to you, love you, or guide you! Either their pleasing beauty will wear off or your eyes will grow dim to their lustre before you are eventually blinded by death. What lasting security can they give to you then? You came from your mother's womb with nothing; you will go to the earth's womb with nothing. How can possessions give you security? You *know* you cannot take them with you.

Riches bring no peace. Sometimes they bring blessings with them, but usually these are reserved for those who have learned to give them away. Riches are more often a burden. They bring insomnia. Few people sleep more peacefully just because they are rich, while many sleep happily knowing only that they have enough. Money cannot buy a mind at rest; it is powerless to quieten a troubled conscience.

Wealth carries no guarantees. It can be amassed to our detriment; it can be lost through misfortune.[1]

Is this what we are destined for as we climb our way up the ladder of success, searching for satisfaction and a sense of significance? The Pundit knew this was a hopeless quest. Something was missing; indeed the one thing essential was missing.

God was missing. The Pundit discovered that the door to fulfilment would not open so long as he had lost the key.

Thankfully, in the course of his memoirs he gives us unmistakable hints that he eventually discovered what the key was:

> *To the man who pleases him, God gives wisdom,*
> *knowledge and happiness . . .*

[1] Eccl. 5:13–14

> *I know that everything God does will endure forever; nothing can be added to it and nothing taken from it. . .*
> *Moreover, when God gives any man wealth and possessions, and enables him to enjoy them, to accept his lot and be happy in his work – this is a gift of God. He seldom reflects on the days of his life, because God keeps him occupied with gladness of heart.* [1]

At one time the Pundit would not have believed that such true contentment was possible in this world. So long as there was no room in his life for God that was bound to be true. But now he had stumbled on the secret. God himself is the secret. As the chronicle of his experiences unfolds this becomes all the clearer. Here is the truth:

> Fading is the worldling's pleasure
> All his boasted pomp and show;
> Solid joys and lasting treasures
> None but Zion's children know.[2]

Is that secret still hidden from you?

I was a very young and inexperienced minister fresh out of college, poorly prepared to deal with life's crises, when my first one was suddenly thrust upon me. At the close of a service a passing stranger in his thirties waited behind to speak to me. He was a person of some means, I discovered; in every ordinary sense a success. But he had just received shattering news about his wife. The unimagined, indeed for him the unimaginable had happened: she had just been told she had cancer.

[1] Eccl. 2:26; 3:14; 5:19
[2] John Newton, 'Glorious things of thee are spoken'

The stranger spoke to me about the success he had made of his life thus far; the possessions he and his wife enjoyed; the resources they had, materially. What were they worth now? There was no emergency account on which to draw for such a time as this; no investment which they could cash in to see them through such a crisis. He had everything most of us would ever want; yet his whole being was crying out for the one thing he now lacked. Like the Pundit his inner soul seemed to cry out, 'Meaningless, meaningless, everything is meaningless'.

I was twenty-three years old at the time; it would have been both foolish and wrong to have pretended that I had ever sat where he was now sitting. But we did talk together about where he could find resources for even such a crisis as this.

I never met the passing stranger again, or discovered whether he found those resources. I have often wondered. But since then I have known men and women in times of similarly desolating emptiness who have found them – and found them where the Pundit did: in God and in all that he is and has done in order to be our God.

No other resources are adequate. Everything else is, ultimately, a chasing after the wind.

2: Life under the Sun

My freedom is the unique foundation of values. And since I am the being by virtue of whom values exist . . . my freedom is in anguish at finding that it is the baseless basis of values.

JEAN-PAUL SARTRE

2

The Pundit had tried just about everything and yet he felt as if he had found nothing. He had certainly not discovered what he was looking for. He knew what the poet Wordsworth meant when he wrote his famous sonnet beginning:

> The world is too much with us; late and soon,
> Getting and spending, we lay waste our powers.

And yet, as we have seen, sometimes he hints that he is watching a re-run of the story of his life – as though he had later learned to look at it with new eyes. There is something more than world-weary cynicism about the way he writes.

In his chronicles, the Pundit's new perspective is indicated by the frequent repetition of the phrase 'under the sun'. He uses it about thirty times in the course of his brief testimony. In a way, the expression underlines that he is looking at life from *inside* the soul of a secular man. From that vantage point this world with its measurable qualities is all there is. Yet there is also the occasional hint that he is no longer the man he once was – but we must be patient and wait for him to tell us more.

He has two questions. The first: What is *the nature of life* under the sun? The second: What is *the meaning of life* under the sun?

THE NATURE OF LIFE

One thing is sure. The Pundit speaks from personal experience: 'I have seen', 'I tested', 'I discovered' are his typical paragraph introductions. But what did he see, test and discover?

An Unfair World

We have an instinctive feeling that things ought to work out fairly. Even some of our common idioms give expression to that: 'fair's fair', or 'fair play' are, for many people, life's essential golden rules. In fact, is that not the essence of the Golden Rule – doing to others what you would like them to do to you?

But open the newspaper: here is a child's life destroyed by an alcoholic driver; here is a teenager sadistically raped; here is someone working no harder than you are, but earning millions. Here are people sullying society with their morally polluting influences, and growing fabulously rich in the process. Why is it such an unequal, even unjust, world?

Several years ago a book by a Jewish rabbi became a best-seller in the United States. Part of the reason for the book's success was almost certainly its title: *When Bad Things Happen to Good People*.

Most people feel that is a moral dilemma which demands an answer. It is not fair or right that life should be like this. There is something here that requires an explanation.

It says a great deal about the way we think about ourselves that the book was not called *When Good Things Happen to Bad People*. Why is that not equally puzzling to us? Why do we take 'good things' for granted, as our right? We are usually more concerned about why it is that *better* things do *not* happen to us.

The Pundit found the injustices of life puzzling and painful too. But he had the wisdom to look at both of these mysteries. He realised that only when we can answer *both* of them have we really found the answer to *either* of them:

> *In this meaningless life of mine I have seen both of these:*
> *a righteous man perishing in his righteousness, and a wicked man living long in his wickedness.*[1]

He sums it up:

> *There is something else meaningless that occurs on earth: righteous men who get what the wicked deserve, and wicked men who get what the righteous deserve. This too, I say, is meaningless.*

He draws the logical, Epicurean, conclusion about life 'under the sun':

> *So I commend the enjoyment of life, because nothing is better for a man under the sun than to eat and drink and be glad.*[2]

In every culture his counsel reappears. If nothing makes sense, then let us eat, drink and be merry, for tomorrow we shall die. *Carpe diem, quam minimum credula postero* wrote the Roman poet Horace: 'Seize the present day; trust tomorrow as little as possible'. Robert Herrick provided the English with their most poetic expression of the same sentiment:

> Gather ye rosebuds while ye may,
> Old Time is still a-flying
> And this same flower that smiles to-day
> To-morrow will be dying.[3]

The Pundit drew the same conclusion:

> *Go, eat your food with gladness, and drink your wine with a joyful heart, for it is now that God favours what you do.*[4]

[1] Eccl. 7:15 [2] Eccl. 8:14-15
[3] From *Hesperides: To the Virgins, to make much of Time* [4] Eccl. 9:7

That may seem like an unexpected confession of faith in the midst of a stream of cynicism. It is not; it is really the expression of a deeper cynicism: enjoy your pleasures while you can; you never know what God – if he exists – may do to you tomorrow.

Is that all that can be said about an unjust topsy-turvy world in answer to the question 'Why do bad things happen to good people?' Yes, indeed, if I am an unbeliever.

In fact, for an unbeliever it is doubtful whether there is any point in asking the question. One distinguished British scientist who is an atheist tells us his response when a child is dying of cancer and his or her parents ask the question 'Why?'. Not only is there no answer, he affirms; this is not an intelligent question to ask. It should not be asked, because it has no answer. There is no more to be said.

However cruel that reply may be, it is certainly logical enough for an atheist. After all, there is no one there to answer. Indeed, there is no ultimate answer. Without God there is no point in asking the question 'Why?', only the question 'How?'. And in that case, we are as well to gather our rosebuds today. Life under the sun is just that – 'under the sun'. When our sun goes down, our end has come; nothing is left. We have no higher significance in ourselves.

Cynical unbelievers sometimes ask the question, 'Why do these things happen if *your* good God exists?' as though the state of the world somehow *destroys* the possibility of faith in God.

The Christian believer is not always able to give full answers to difficult questions. But the situation of unbelievers is more desperate: their whole being cries out to ask a question which their refusal and rejection of God renders illegitimate. If there is no God, there is no *ultimate* answer to the question 'Why?'. There is no one there to answer our cries; there is no 'meaning' to life – there is only life itself.

But the fact that the question 'Why?' persists in our

minds and hearts suggests that the echoes of God's revelation have not been finally silenced. The unbeliever asks it too, and discovers that his or her own being seems to be at cross purposes with the world-and-life view of atheism. The truth is as Paul says: he or she must suppress and repress the truth about God. The unbeliever must deny what he or she knows to be true.[1]

Eventually it would dawn on the Pundit how to answer the question 'Why do bad things happen to good people?'. The short form of the answer is in two parts:

1. There are no 'good people':

> *There is no one righteous, not even one;*
> *there is no one who understands,*
> *no one who seeks God.*
> *All have turned away . . .*
> *there is no one who does good,*
> *not even one.*[2]

2. The real mystery, therefore, is: 'Why do *good* things happen to people who are not good?'. The fundamental difference between the biblical world-view and all others is summed up in this: we feel we should have the good things we deserve; the biblical world-view teaches us that we do not *deserve* anything good; we have forfeited all claims to it.

The Pundit recognised something else.

Unreliable People

He lost his ability to trust others. That happened for various reasons. You cannot put any absolute trust in what people say. You cannot trust what people do. You cannot fully trust those who work for you:

[1] See Romans 1:18ff. [2] Rom. 3:10-12.

Do not pay attention to every word people say
or you may hear your servant cursing you –

How does he know this?

for you know in your heart
that many times you yourself have cursed
others.[1]

The outside world, he realised, was just a reflection of the world inside: it was unreliable. But, then, so was he.

Now he was beginning to get nearer to the heart of the matter. Yet he adds a further subtle twist. Bad enough when those who work for you are unreliable; even worse to discover that he was similarly twisted himself. But what he now discovers is that even those he finds attractive are unreliable.

Part of what attracts us to people is a sense that we can trust them. We want those we find congenial to be trustworthy, because we want to be able to rely on them. That, of course, is particularly true in an intimate personal relationship between a man and a woman.

But listen to the Pundit:

I find more bitter than death
the woman who is a snare,
whose heart is a trap
and whose hands are chains.
The man who pleases God will escape her,
but the sinner she will ensnare.
'Look', . . . 'this is what I have discovered:
Adding one thing to another to discover the scheme
of things –
while I was still searching but not finding –

[1] Eccl. 7:21–22

I found one upright man among a thousand,
but not one upright woman among them all.
This only have I found:
God made mankind upright,
but men have gone in search of many schemes'.[1]

The Pundit's comments here are not those of a misogynist, a disappointed and twisted woman-hater. He is speaking here from a male standpoint. After all, he is a man! It does not take much imagination to guess what these comments might have been if the Pundit had been a woman! In any event, he 'found one upright man among a thousand, but not one upright woman among them all'.

There is not much difference between finding only one man in a thousand and finding no woman in a thousand who is upright. Did the Pundit think of himself as the one exception? It is interesting how many of us, in our disappointment with the failures of others, begin to wonder if we ourselves are the only one who can be trusted – the one in a thousand!

What is it that disappoints him? It is something which the creators of our advertisements recognise instinctively, even if they never articulate it to the public, or are consciously aware of it: *we all have a native tendency to infidelity*. We cannot be trusted; we are also deceived when we regard ourselves as altogether reliable.

The Pundit had experienced an unmasking which sobered him deeply: behind the appearance of attractiveness and trustworthiness lies a deceitful and unsubdued unreliability. Of course we use language which will disguise the truth, especially in the context of human relationships. We speak today of 'affairs' rather than of adultery; of 'love' when we mean 'lust'; of 'magnetic attraction', when in fact we are

[1] Eccl. 7:26–28

engaging in theft – stealing another's wife or husband. Men and women who would be horrified to be accused of cheating or of stealing have no qualms about both cheating and theft when it comes to human relationships. Guilty of both, men and women hide it only by means of false-description.

Perhaps the Pundit had once assumed that infidelity was a small blemish in a good man or woman. Now he saw things more clearly. Infidelity is not a deviation from our otherwise true self; it is a revelation of our real nature. We are, literally, infidels. Unfaithful to the God who created us it is hardly surprising if we prove to be unfaithful in the relationships he made for us.

Nor is this unreliability and infidelity limited to relationships between the sexes. What is true of that fundamental relationship pervades all relationships. It is not simply a matter of the *femme fatale*, but of the fatal flaw in the character of each of us.

For the Pundit this discovery was a shattering blow. But there was still more to come.

Irrational Future

The future is certainly unpredictable:

> *Since no man knows the future,*
> *who can tell him what is to come?*[1]

Of this he is sure:

> *When times are good, be happy;*
> *but when times are bad, consider:*
> *God has made the one as well as the other.*
> *Therefore, a man cannot discover*
> *anything about his future.*
> *No one knows what is coming –*
> *who can tell him what will happen after him?*[2]

[1] Eccl. 8:7 [2] Eccl. 7:14; 10:14b

What is worse, the future seems to be completely irrational as well as unpredictable:

> *Whoever digs a pit may fall into it;*
> *whoever breaks through a wall may be bitten by a snake.*
> *Whoever quarries stones may be injured by them;*
> *whoever splits logs may be endangered by them.*

He adds, with a touch of wry humour:

> *If a snake bites before it is charmed,*
> *there is no profit for the charmer.*[1]

There is neither rhyme nor reason to either the events of history or the experiences of the individual. In this life we can be certain of very little. Everything is the result of time plus chance, nothing more. There is no answer to the question 'why?' only to the question 'how?':

> *I have seen something else*
> *under the sun:*
> *The race is not to the swift*
> *or the battle to the strong,*
> *nor does food come to the wise*
> *or wealth to the brilliant*
> *or favour to the learned;*
> *but time and chance happen to them all.*[2]

It is hard to believe the Pundit was one of the ancients, for here he speaks as a thoroughly sophisticated modern man! We are all products of chance events working. Life is, as the Latin author Lucretius (95–45 BC) said, simply a fortuitous concourse of atoms after all. Throwing the dice of chance long enough and frequently enough turns the primeval slime

[1] Eccl. 10:8–9, 11 [2] Eccl. 9:11

into a Shakespeare, mud into a Milton; but it may also turn into a Nebuchadnezzar, a Genghis Khan or a Hitler – you can never be sure. Genius, saint and tyrant alike turn out to be freaks of nature. Indeed, on this view of life, we are all freaks of nature, the good as well as the evil.

There is an uncannily contemporary ring to what the Pundit is saying. Imagining himself to be too sophisticated intellectually to believe in God, modern man speaks of 'time and chance' and of 'Mother Nature' (notice the capital letters!). God is naturalised, nature is deified. We rid ourselves of God, but in the process substitute another, poorer deity in his place, becoming indeed the children of a lesser god. We become just like our long-dead forefathers whose gods were also found in nature.

Our popular and best-selling newspapers and the morning magazine programmes on television provide one of the most amazing illustrations of this, given modern man's much vaunted rejection of the Christian tradition. Daily space and time are given to astrologers to guide our lives into the future; little, if any, space is given to Christian ministers to guide us into eternity. Having given up the faith of our fathers, professedly for many people, because of what 'science' is believed to have 'proved', we believe in the stars! Having rejected the Bible as our guide, we take our guidance from the astrologers instead!

In view of this it is unnerving to read Paul's two-stage view of spiritual declension:

(i) the truth about God is exchanged for a lie;
(ii) the creation is worshipped instead of the Creator.

> *They exchanged the truth of God for a lie, and worshipped and served created things rather than the Creator . . .* [1]

[1] Rom. 1:25

When we cease to believe in God we begin to believe in nature instead. We were made to believe, to trust in Another. But if we cease to believe in the Creator we begin to believe in anything.

Life 'under the sun' – that is life seen without taking the presence and purposes of God into account – is just a series of throws of the dice; that is all there is.

An Inevitable End

Death, the Great Leveller, the Grim Reaper – call it what we will – meets us all at the end. This is the final inevitability. But it is also the great uncertainty.

Here is Shakespeare's Hamlet contemplating his end:

> To die: to sleep;
> No more; and by a sleep to say we end
> The heart-ache and the thousand natural shocks
> That flesh is heir to, 'tis a consummation
> Devoutly to be wished. To die, to sleep:
> To sleep: perchance to dream: ay there's the rub;
> For in that sleep of death what dreams may come
> When we have shuffled off this mortal coil,
> Must gives us pause . . .
>   the dread of something after death
> The undiscover'd country from whose bourn
> No traveller returns, puzzles the will
> And makes us rather bear those ills we have
> Than fly to others that we know not of?[1]

And here, centuries before, yet similarly, is the Pundit:

> *No man knows whether love or hate awaits him. All share a common destiny – the righteous and the wicked, the good and the bad, the clean and the*

[1] *Hamlet*, III.i.

unclean, those who offer sacrifices and those who do not.

As it is with the good man,
so it is with the sinner;
as it is with those who take oaths,
so with those who are afraid to take them.

This is the evil in everything that happens under the sun: The same destiny overtakes all.

The hearts of men, moreover, are full of evil and there is madness in their hearts while they live, and afterward they join the dead. Anyone who is among the living has hope – even a live dog is better off than a dead lion!

For the living know that they will die,
but the dead know nothing;
they have no further reward,
and even the memory of them is forgotten . . .

And so he sums up:

Whatever your hand finds to do, do it with all your might, for in the grave, where you are going,
there is neither working nor planning nor knowledge nor wisdom.[1]

In fact, the situation is even bleaker for the Pundit than it was for poor Hamlet. Death is a life-destroying icy blast which freezes all hope. The great inevitability, it also produces great uncertainty. It wears the mask of a mocker. It comes equally to all, the righteous and the unrighteous, the rich and the poor, and thus makes nonsense of all of life's distinctions:

[1] Eccl. 9:1–10

The wise man has eyes in his head,
while the fool walks in the darkness;
but I came to realise
that the same fate overtakes them both
Then I thought in my heart,
'The fate of the fool will overtake me also.
What then do I gain by being wise?'
I said in my heart,
'This too is meaningless.'
For the wise man, like the fool, will not be long remembered;
in days to come both will be forgotten.
Like the fool, the wise man too must die![1]

Like the Bible,[2] he sees there is only one logical conclusion to life if it has no post-mortem hope, no promise of a resurrection: Let us eat, drink and be merry. Tomorrow we die. 'Meaningless, everything is meaningless'.

Recognising this is not a matter of great intellectual powers, or of superior analytical judgement. It is no more than a matter of honest thinking. The Pundit was no doubt a brilliant man; but he is not speaking here as a genius, only as a simple realist who has faced up to the ultimate truth about 'life under the sun'. It ends. Without God, this is all there is. We must make the best we can of it.

No wonder there is a thick and strong thread of cynicism woven into the central section of the Pundit's chronicle. Having unmasked his own enormous capacity for self-deceit, he sees that without God he is only earth-dust, and to earth-dust he will return. He was nothing; he will come to nothing.

But one question remains: Is he really able to take that in and live in the light of it? Can he seriously face up to the fact of his death as one more meaningless event in an endless flow

[1] Eccl. 2:14–16 [2] Isaiah 22:13; 1 Corinthians 15:32

of meaningless events? And further, can he live consistently with that fact? Can he forever silence the cries, which arise from every facet of his being, that there *must* be more to life than this?

Only if he can find an explanation for those deep and instinctive longings.

THE MEANING OF LIFE

The Pundit is an engagingly honest figure and it is hard not to like him. We are bound to ask: did he discover meaning to life?

The answer comes in stages, but long before the conclusion to his chronicles he hints that he has found a clue:

> *This only have I found:*
> *God made mankind upright,*
> *but men have gone in search of many schemes.*[1]

He gives little indication as to how this dawned on him, but his words are obviously a personal testimony. At some point he must have realised that there *is* an explanation for the apparent meaninglessness of life. He had come to it only slowly because it had involved him in the personal pain of questioning the basis of his entire life. He had made a serious mistake in his thinking; now he had to undo it. It was not easy; but he knew it had to be done.

The Pundit's error was to begin from the wrong starting point. All his thinking presupposed that his spiritual condition was normal. But the truth is that we are all spiritually abnormal; we are diseased, broken and twisted.

Man was made by God as his image; he was created in order to reflect the character of God in a miniature way in this world.[2] He was created to live in fellowship with God and in service to him; to understand God's ways and to enjoy

[1] Eccl. 7:29 [2] Gen. 1:26-27

his presence. Instead he turned away from God, broke his laws, despised his love, and tried to seize independence. He thus marred his personal life and introduced a distortion into the world in general as well as into his own posterity. Things went wrong, both in the world of nature and the world of human experience. This is what the Pundit began to see:

> *There is not a righteous man on earth*
> *who does what is right and never sins.*[1]

Here is the root of the problem: human sin.

> *This is the evil in everything that happens under*
> *the sun: The same destiny overtakes all.*
> *The hearts of men, moreover, are full of evil and*
> *there is madness in their hearts while they live,*
> *and afterward they join the dead.*[2]

We were made for greatness and glory; but we have developed deep flaws. As a result we cannot think clearly about God or about our relationship to him. No wonder the Pundit began to feel that everything was meaningless; his thinking about everything had begun from the wrong starting point.

One of the most famous works ever written in the Christian church is still usually referred to by its Latin title *Cur Deus Homo*, Why did God become man? Written by Anselm of Canterbury (1033–1109), it takes the form of a dialogue between Anselm and his young student, Boso. In keeping with the impression suggested by Boso's name, he is rather slow on the uptake. But this gives Anselm the opportunity to explain the Christian faith in simple and vivid ways.

In one of the most famous passages in the book, Anselm vigorously responds to Boso's questions by saying: '*You have not yet considered the greatness of the weight of sin*'.[3]

[1] Eccl. 7:20 [2] Eccl. 9:3 [3] Anselm, *Cur Deus Homo*, I.xxi

That tendency is characteristic of the way we all think – without taking account of our own basic sinfulness. We imagine that our minds operate in a spiritually and morally neutral way. If we think of sin at all we see it as 'something' in the world outside of ourselves. The truth, however, is that sin is so enfolded within our beings that we do not detect its presence dominating the ways in which we think and feel about everything. So long as that is the case we can never begin to understand why the world is as it is.

Here is a New Testament Christian's searing analysis:

> *Although they knew God, they neither glorified him as God nor gave thanks to him, but their thinking became futile and their foolish hearts were darkened. Although they claimed to be wise, they became fools.*[1]

But the Pundit had already hinted that he was coming to see the truth:

> *I have seen the burden God has laid on men.*
> *He has made everything beautiful in its time.*
> *He has also set eternity in the hearts of men; yet they cannot fathom what God has done from beginning to end.*[2]

He realised that the frustration he felt at his inability to make sense of things on his own was actually the result of a God-given burden. God created a world of beauty in space and time; but he also made us to know him and to live in his presence; he thus set eternity and a desire for it in our hearts. Consequently, we can never be finally satisfied with anything the world can offer us. Made as God's image, created for him, we must remain forever dissatisfied until we live in

[1] Rom. 1:21–22 [2] Eccl. 3:10–11

fellowship with him and for his glory. We were made for eternity, not merely for time; we were made for God's presence, not merely for life in the space-time continuum. No wonder, then, if there is confusion and frustration when we turn away from him. It should not surprise us that, if we choose to live in the dark, we cannot see.

But sin does more than frustrate; it makes us fugitives from our destiny. Yet in our sinfulness we remain plagued by a sense of homesickness. Nothing in this world can ever relieve us of that pain.

According to the New Testament, there is no escape from the knowledge of God, even if I am an unbeliever. I may seek to repress it, but I cannot escape it. There are no ultimate atheists, only theists who argue against what, in the deepest recesses of their being, they know to be true: God is. We cannot succeed in our struggle permanently to suppress that knowledge. We certainly cannot do so consistently. This is God's world, and all who live in it must borrow from God's capital in order to do so.

The principle of humanism – this material world is all there is – does not and cannot account for the way things actually are, or for what we ourselves are. In fact, if you listen carefully to the western humanist, you will frequently find him or her borrowing from the capital of the Christian faith, its concepts and language, in order to give any kind of coherency to life. Why is this? It is because the famous words in which Augustine echoed the Pundit are still true:

> You have made us for yourself
> and our hearts are restless
> until they find their rest in you.[1]

There is nowhere else to go, no other fountain from which

[1] Augustine, *Confessions*, I.i.

we can drink if we are to quench our thirst. God alone can do that.

We will see that the Pundit has much more to teach us. But for the moment we should pause to reflect on what he is saying. Consider how great the weight of your sin is.

3: Wisdom from the Poor Man

The true problem lies in the
hearts and thoughts of men . . .
What terrifies us is not the explosive
force of the atomic bomb, but the
power of the wickedness of the human heart.

ALBERT EINSTEIN

3

The Pundit was a man of wide experience. He was also a man with strong appetites. Not for him the half-hearted search for truth! He was prepared to try anything; yet he was invariably disappointed. Nothing in the world seemed to deliver what it promised.

Yet, even at his cynical low points he had fleeting moments of illumination penetrating the darkness of his world. He was like a man lost in a labyrinth pursuing beams of light in the hope that one of them would lead him out into the rays of the sun. Life is like that for everyone – even the committed agnostic and atheist. There is no escape from the flickering moments which make us feel that we are being haunted by the shadow of God.

Robert Browning's marvellous and intriguingly-entitled poem, *Bishop Blaugram's Apology*, captures this perfectly. Browning portrays the bishop being interviewed by an unlikely-named journalist called Gigadibs who questions him confidently about his doubts. No modern man would believe the traditional orthodoxies. Surely the bishop does not really believe?

Bishop Blaugram retorts that, in effect, the boot is on the other foot:

> So you despise me, Mr Gigadibs . . .
>   how can we guard our unbelief
> Make it bear fruit for us? – the problem here.

Just when we are safest, there's a sunset touch,
A fancy from a flower-bell, some one's death,
A chorus ending from Euripides, –
And that's enough for fifty hopes and fears
As old and new at once as Nature's self,
To rap and knock and enter in our soul,
Take hands and dance there, a fantastic ring . . .

God has planted testimonies to his presence throughout life; there is no safe-haven in any part of creation; no exit door through which we can permanently escape from the reality of his creating and sustaining power.

So it was for the Pundit. Moments of illumination made him question his doubts. This happened on one occasion in particular. He saw something that impressed him; yet responses to it left him puzzled and mystified:

I also saw under the sun this example of wisdom that greatly impressed me: There was once a small city with only a few people in it. And a powerful king came against it, surrounded it and built huge siegeworks against it.
Now there lived in that city a man poor but wise, and he saved the city by his wisdom. But nobody remembered that poor man. So I said 'Wisdom is better than strength.' But the poor man's wisdom is despised, and his words are no longer heeded.[1]

Clearly he felt that there was something deeply puzzling about this. Here was a man who seemed to be able to meet the needs of society and save it. Yet the response to him was an inexplicable indifference. The saving actions of the poor but wise man brought hope; yet he had been forgotten. Why?

[1] Eccl. 9:13–16

The words read almost like a prophecy. Whose name most naturally comes to mind when we hear of a poor man, full of wisdom, who became a saviour but whose life and teaching have been neglected and rejected?

Instinctively we think of Jesus. The man the Pundit saw had the attributes of true spirituality and wisdom; but he was just a reflection, a kind of preview of the spirituality and wisdom of the true Poor and Wise Man who would later become a Saviour.

The New Testament actually talks about Jesus in precisely these terms. Paul describes him as 'Christ the . . . wisdom of God.'[1] He summarises the meaning of his life and death: 'though he was rich, yet for your sakes he became poor, so that you through his poverty might become rich'.[2]

The Pundit sought true wisdom, but could not find it. How, then, is true wisdom to be found in Jesus Christ? In these different ways:

JESUS' IDENTITY

The opening verses of John's Gospel describe Jesus as the Word or *Logos* of God. They stress that the Jesus whose story the Gospel tells did not have his origin in time; he was 'in the beginning with God and . . . was God'.

The background to these words lies partly in an eloquent Old Testament description of God's Wisdom. In Proverbs 8, Wisdom is made to speak as though it had a personal identity. It was present with God and took part in the original creation:

> *I was appointed from eternity,*
> *from the beginning before the world began . . .*
> *I was there when he set the heavens in place,*
> *when he marked out the horizon on*
> *the face of the deep . . .*

[1] 1 Cor. 1:24 [2] 2 Cor. 8:9.

Then I was the craftsman at his side.
I was filled with delight day after day,
rejoicing always in his presence,
rejoicing in his whole world
and delighting in mankind.[1]

Of course, Wisdom is not a person; this is simply a figure of speech. John knew this, but he gave it a special twist: while Wisdom is not a person, there is a person who is Wisdom. That person is Jesus.

Like Wisdom in the Book of Proverbs, Jesus, the Word of God was active in creation: 'Through him all things were made; without him nothing was made that has been made'.[2]

As the Wisdom of God, the Word of God is uncreated: 'In the beginning was the Word, and the Word was with God, and the Word was God . . . without him nothing was made that has been made'.[3] There is an eternal person who is wisdom – in everything he is, says and does. More than that, this Wisdom or *Logos* 'became flesh and made his dwelling among us. We have seen his glory, the glory of the One and Only, who came from the Father, full of grace and truth.'[4]

Jesus is the wisdom of God made flesh – wisdom in human form and experience.

He is wisdom *in human form*. The wisdom Jesus displayed was not that of a pre-programmed computerised mind; he had to learn it as he grew up from childhood to adulthood:

The child grew and became strong; he was filled with wisdom . . .
And Jesus grew in wisdom and stature . . .[5]

[1] Proverbs 8:23–31 [2] John 1:3 [3] John 1:1–3
[4] John 1:14 [5] Luke 2:40, 52

How did he do that? Apparently by the way he learned and applied to his life the teaching of God's written word in the Old Testament.

Here is God's wisdom indeed! It does not come to us emblazoned in the skies high above us, nor in recondite works of philosophical and scientific learning; but in teaching which even as a youngster Jesus could discuss and understand.[1] He learned God's wisdom and exemplified it in human flesh and blood. Wisdom was revealed in a Word

> *which we have heard, which we have seen with our eyes, which we have looked at and our hands have touched . . .*
> *The life appeared; we have seen it and testify to it, and we proclaim to you the eternal life, which was with the Father and has appeared to us.*[2]

We could never hope even to begin to understand the naked truth about God's wisdom; but God has shown it to us in a way we can grasp, sending his Son to take our human nature and in it to display true wisdom.

JESUS' TEACHING

We need only to read the story of Jesus' life and the account of his teaching to see that here we have the way of wisdom; any other pattern of lifestyle is folly. But, as with the poor man whom the Pundit saw, to follow Christ's wisdom hurts and costs.

We still hear it said: 'If only people would live by the Sermon on the Mount, the world would be a completely different and infinitely better place.' True, of course. Think how much of your tax contribution would be unnecessary if

[1] See Luke 2:41–50 [2] 1 John 1:1–2

there were no theft, no dishonesty, no need for police, little need for law courts, no defence budget! Even insurance policies would be cheaper.

But the wisdom in Jesus' teaching goes deeper than outlining a manifesto for better living. For our problem is not merely our failure to observe better behaviour patterns. It is not what happens on the outside, either in our behaviour or in the structures of society that ultimately lets us down. The problem lies deep within. Jesus' wise teaching penetrates our vague and often superficial thinking to unveil the unwelcome truth that the fatal sickness lies within our own hearts and minds: they love the wrong things, they are morally polluted and they are ruled by sin:

> *You have heard that it was said, 'Do not commit adultery.' But I tell you that anyone who looks at a woman lustfully has already committed adultery with her in his heart.*
>
> *The evil man brings evil things out of the evil stored up in his heart. For out of the overflow of his heart his mouth speaks.*
>
> *But the things that come out of the mouth come from the heart, and these make a man 'unclean'. For out of the heart come evil thoughts, murder, adultery, sexual immorality, theft, false testimony, slander.*
> *These are what make a man 'unclean'.*[1]

We begin to make progress towards true wisdom only when we realise that we have a major heart defect which, unless remedied, will prove spiritually fatal.

[1] Mattthew 5:27–28; Luke 6:45; Matt. 15:18–20

JESUS' WORK

According to the New Testament, the way in which the wisdom of God is most clearly demonstrated is in the death of Jesus.

That may seem completely incomprehensible. Humanly speaking Jesus' death was a tragic miscarriage of justice. How can we see in it the divine *wisdom*? Even the loyal apostle Paul admitted that his message about 'Christ crucified . . . [was] a stumbling block to Jews and foolishness to Gentiles.'[1]

How, then, is wisdom to be seen in the death of Christ? In this: it demonstrates both the love and justice of God.

Through the cross God does two things which are otherwise impossible:

(i) He pardons those who believe in Christ, although they have sinned and deserve only condemnation. Without this we would be excluded forever from his presence.

(ii) He displays and satisfies his perfect and holy justice by executing the punishment our sins deserve. Without this God would not be true to himself.

We have sinned. We deserve punishment for our sins. But God sent his Son to become one of us. He lived a life of perfect obedience and holiness. He had no sins for which to be condemned. He voluntarily accepted the condemnation we deserve.

Jesus spoke about the cross long before either the Jews or the Romans condemned him to die. He had known for a long time that this was the cup which his Father had sent him to drink.[2]

This is why, shortly before his death, as he prayed in the Garden of Gethsemane, he was almost overcome. He was almost beside himself with the horror of what he was about

[1] 1 Cor. 1:23 [2] See Mark 10:38–39

to experience and asked God if there was any other possible way to deliver his people:

> *He . . . began to be deeply distressed and troubled.*
> *'My soul is overwhelmed with sorrow to the point of death,' he said to them . . .*
> *Going a little farther, he fell to the ground and prayed that if possible the hour might pass from him. 'Abba, Father,' he said, 'everything is possible for you. Take this cup from me.*
> *Yet not what I will, but what you will.'* [1]

But there was no other way; and so he drank the cup.

The Bible leaves us in no doubt what that cup was. The writings of the prophets refer to it as the cup of God's judgement and wrath against sinners. Here is a sampling of its contents:

> *Awake, awake! . . . you who have drunk from the hand of the Lord the cup of his wrath . . . the goblet that makes men stagger . . .*
> *the cup that made you stagger; from that cup, the goblet of my wrath . . .*
>
> *This is what the Lord . . . said to me: 'Take from my hand this cup filled with the wine of my wrath and make all the nations to whom I send you drink it. When they drink it, they will stagger and go mad . . .'*
> *So I took the cup . . . and made all the nations . . . drink it . . . to make them a ruin and an object of horror and scorn and cursing . . .*

[1] Mark 14:33–36

You will drink . . . a cup large and deep;
it will bring scorn and derision . . . the cup of ruin and desolation . . .
You will be filled with shame instead of glory. Now it is your turn! Drink and be exposed! The cup from the Lord's right hand is coming around to you, and disgrace will cover your glory.[1]

On the night on which Jesus was arrested, the temperature in Jerusalem dropped so low that Simon Peter risked being identified as a disciple of Jesus by trying to warm himself by a fire in the courtyard of the High Priest's house.[2] Yet Jesus' anguish in the Garden of Gethsemane was so intense that 'his sweat was like drops of blood falling to the ground'.[3]

Why such sweat on a cold night? Was Jesus afraid? Afraid to die, perhaps? Not in the sense of fearing an unknown or uncertain afterlife. Afraid of the pain of dying by crucifixion? That would be a natural human reaction; crucifixion surely qualifies as cruel and unnatural punishment.

But there is a deeper reason. It was not merely the cup of crucifixion, the physical experience of dying in pain, Jesus feared. It was the contents of the 'cup' which made him tremble: the wrath of God, the sense of horror at bearing our sin and guilt into his holy presence and coming under the curse of God's covenant. Jesus' holy humanity must have been overawed when he contemplated the shame and the inner pain of feeling abandoned by his Father.

This was the meaning of Jesus' death; this *is* the real meaning of death. Martin Luther was surely right to say about Jesus: 'No man ever feared death like this man.' Death as 'the wages of sin' (as the Bible calls it[4]) is what Jesus

[1] Isa. 51:17, 22; Jeremiah 25:15–18; Ezekiel 23:32–33; Habakkuk 2:16
[2] See John 18:25 [3] Luke 22:44 [4] Rom. 6:23

feared because it meant not only the disintegration of his life, but alienation from God. That sense of being absolutely forsaken by his Father, isolation, darkness, desolation, is what lies behind the cry from the cross with which he pierced the sunless Friday afternoon of the Passover weekend: 'My God, my God, why have you forsaken me?'[1]

Where is the wisdom of God here? It is found in this: God's incarnate Son has identified himself with us in such a way that he is able to represent us, indeed substitute himself in our place before God's judgement and under his wrath. He changes places with us, takes the guilt of our sin to himself, and accepts the divine judgement against us. On the cross he bore the full weight of God's wrath. His Father turned his face away from him. In the outward darkness of Golgotha, the Son of God experienced the inner darkness of his own Father's rejection. Utterly alone he entered the dark night of death as sin's penalty. He bore that for us.

Yet here the divine master-stroke appears. Because he was the *incarnate* Son of God, he was able to die as one of us in our place. But because he was the perfect and holy *Son of God*, death did not have the power to restrain him in its grip. The wisdom of God was seen in this: what appeared at first to be a human tragedy – Jesus' death – was, in fact, the key to the divine strategy and the prelude to his resurrection.

This is such a central part of the gospel that it became a major theme in the first Christian sermon. Said Peter:

Men of Israel, listen to this: Jesus of Nazareth
was a man accredited by God to you by miracles,
wonders and signs, which God did among you
through him, as you yourselves know.
This man was handed over to you by God's set
purpose and foreknowledge; and you, with the
help of wicked men, put him to death by nailing

[1] Matt. 27:46

him to the cross. But God raised him from the
dead, freeing him from the agony of death,
because it was impossible for death to keep its hold
on him.[1]

Christ has been raised – that is the message. His death was actually the stepping stone to his triumph and victory.

Furthermore, in this same sermon on the Day of Pentecost, Peter explains what Christ has done. He has fulfilled his promise to send his Spirit to his disciples, to help them to understand the significance of his work, and to fill their lives with his grace and power to enable them to live for him.[2]

Because Christ died for us, those who trust in him may know that their guilt has been pardoned once-and-for-all. Because Christ is risen those who trust him may know his presence and live in fellowship with him. Because he sends his Spirit to his people, those who trust him can grow in his wisdom and live in his power.

AN ANSWER FOR THE PUNDIT

Here, at last, is the answer to the Pundit's search.

In Jesus Christ, says Paul (who formerly resisted the idea with all his considerable powers), we find all the treasures of wisdom and knowledge.[3] He is the Wise Man, and in him alone is true wisdom to be found. He is the Poor Man whose impoverishment leads to untold riches for those who trust him.

Even in the days of the Old Testament, the coming Saviour had been portrayed in precisely these terms. Isaiah was given this divine vision of him:

A shoot will come up from the stump of
Jesse [David's family];
from his roots a Branch will bear fruit.

[1] Acts 2:22–24 [2] See John 14:25–31; Acts 1:8 [3] Colossians 2:3

The Spirit of the Lord will rest on him –
the Spirit of wisdom and of understanding . . .
the Spirit of knowledge and of
the fear of the Lord –
and he will delight in the fear of the Lord.

See, my servant will act wisely . . .

He was despised and rejected by men,
a man of sorrows, and familiar with suffering.
Like one from whom men hide their faces
he was despised
and we esteemed him not.[1]

The first Christians all believed that these words, and the entire passage in the Old Testament from which they come (Isaiah 52:13–53:12), were a prophecy of the life and work of Jesus and were ultimately fulfilled in him.

The evidence for this statement is remarkably full. Almost every verse from the passage is cited or alluded to in the New Testament, with clear reference to Jesus. Two examples will help us to see the relevance of this prophecy.

The death of Stephen, the first Christian martyr, signalled the outbreak of a wave of persecution against the young church in Jerusalem. Christians scattered throughout Judea and Samaria in order to save their lives. Philip, a colleague of Stephen, fled to Samaria where he began to preach with extraordinary results. Peter and John even visited to see exactly what was happening.

In the midst of these already remarkable events, Philip had a further unusual experience. Under a deep sense of divine compulsion he made his way, alone, to the desert road which led from Jerusalem to Gaza. As he travelled he met up with the distinguished Court Treasurer of Ethiopia, travelling home by chariot after a visit to Jerusalem. Amazingly – since

[1] Isa. 11:1–2; 52:13, 53:3

it must have been expensive to obtain – he had a copy of Isaiah's prophecy with him and was reading from it – out loud, as was the custom. In fact, he was in the process of reading Isaiah 53 when Philip met him!

Philip asked him if he understood the passage of Scripture he was reading. 'I don't think I will be able to, unless someone explains it to me,' replied the eunuch, inviting Philip to join him in the chariot in the hope that he might be able to help. The scroll of Isaiah lay open at these words:

He was led like a sheep to the slaughter,
and as a lamb before her shearers is silent,
so he did not open his mouth.
In his humiliation he was deprived of justice.
Who can speak of his descendants?
For his life was taken from the earth.[1]

'Was the prophet talking here about himself or about somebody else?' the eunuch asked. That was the very question Philip must have hoped he would hear. Beginning with Isaiah 53 he began to explain to him the good news: Isaiah was talking about Jesus![2]

Jesus was the Suffering Servant. Charged with the twin crimes of blasphemy and treason he had remained as silent as a lamb. He had been led to the slaughter, although even those who condemned him had over and over again pronounced him innocent.[3] The passage in Isaiah explained why:

He was pierced for our transgressions,
he was crushed for our iniquities;
the punishment that brought us peace
was upon him
and by his wounds we are healed.

[1] Isa. 53:7–8, quoted in Acts 8:32–33 [2] Acts 8:30–35
[3] See Luke 23:4, 14, 15, 22, 40–41, 47 for repeated statements that Jesus was innocent, although he was condemned.

> *We all, like sheep, have gone astray,*
> *each of us has turned to his own way;*
> *and the Lord has laid on him*
> *the iniquity of us all.*[1]

This Ethiopian man was *en route* home from a visit to Jerusalem. His background was probably typical of such pilgrims from distant lands. Dissatisfied with the traditional religion of his own country he (or perhaps his family before him) had come into contact with the Jewish faith and had been attracted by its emphasis on one, true and living God, by its moral wholesomeness, by its promise of a coming Saviour, and by the wisdom of its Scriptures.

But what was on his mind as he made his way back to his native land after this great pilgrimage to the Holy City? And why was he reading Isaiah 53, the very passage to which the early Christians always turned when they spoke about Jesus of Nazareth?

No doubt God's hand is to be detected in this 'coincidence'. But clearly this man was searching for something he did not yet know or possess. Perhaps having already become dissatisfied with his native religion, he had now begun to feel that there was something still missing, or at least incomplete, in the ritual of the animal sacrifices he had witnessed in Jerusalem. Yes, they were offered for his sins, and so they seemed to point towards peace with God. But they needed to be repeated day after day. Surely, then, they could not really be taking his guilt away permanently? Despite the excitement of the pilgrimage, he was going home with unanswered questions. This strange figure of whom Isaiah spoke, for example, this Servant of God who would deal with sin and guilt once and for all – who was he? What did Isaiah mean when he said that he would be 'pierced for our transgressions' and 'crushed for our iniquities'?

[1] Isa. 53:5–6

Isaiah had good news for him: God would do something to deal with failure to keep the law ('transgressions') and the twisted element in the human heart ('iniquities'). Here, at last, was hope. But of whom did Isaiah speak?

It seems that God had been preparing him for this moment when Philip would explain to him that Jesus was the Suffering Servant and Saviour. The Ethiopian believed, was baptised into the Christian church and returned home rejoicing.[1] At last he had found the wisdom he had sought, but until now never discovered. God's way of providing salvation required Jesus' death.

During Jesus' ministry, Simon Peter had struggled against this. It would break the fisherman's heart if his Master were to suffer. The very idea terrified him. For if Jesus were to die, what would happen to his closest followers? Peter tried to resist the thought that the path ahead was covered with suffering and even with the blood of sacrifice. When Jesus himself began to speak more openly about it, Peter cornered and rebuked his Master in his desperate anxiety to prevent him going to the cross.[2] Only later did he come to see that there was no other way by which Jesus could become the Saviour. Then, at last, Peter was able to write:

> *'He committed no sin,*
> *and no deceit was found*
> *in his mouth'.* [cited from Isaiah 53:9]
> *When they hurled their insults at him, he did not retaliate; when he suffered, he made no threats. Instead, he entrusted himself to him who judges justly. He himself bore our sins in his body on the tree, so that we might die to sins and live for righteousness; by his wounds you have been healed.*

[1] Acts 8:26–40 [2] Matt.16:21–23

> *For you were like sheep going astray, but now you have returned to the Shepherd and Overseer of your souls.*[1]

Our ultimate folly lies in our sinfulness. Consequently, guilt is our great problem. But it is not a problem which psychiatrists can solve; guilt-feelings, perhaps; real guilt, no. Only God can solve the problem of real guilt, since our guilt arises from our sin against him.

Sin is folly, because it is disobedience to and rebellion against the will of the One who has made us, loves us, sustains us and will finally assess us. What could be more foolish than that? Even worse than being foolish, it also alienates us from God. More, it places us under his condemnation; it exposes us to danger, to his wrath which is 'revealed from heaven against all the godlessness and wickedness of men who suppress the truth by their wickedness'.[2]

But God has provided the way of salvation in Jesus Christ. He reveals his love and justice, but also meets our needs precisely. What love! Yes, and what wisdom!

The Pundit could not erase from his mind the realisation that the poor man whom he had seen save the city was the only truly wise man; but he could not understand why he had been ignored. He was like a man caught in a blackout whose torch flickers on momentarily before the battery goes dead. He knew he had seen something important – but what was it, and what did it mean?

The New Testament helps us to understand. God's Son, his Wisdom, became poor for us so that we might become truly rich through him.[3] Through Christ we may become rich in wisdom, because at last we understand our foolishness and know where truth is to be found; rich in peace,

[1] 1 Peter 2:22-25 [2] Rom. 1:18 [3] See 2 Cor. 8:9

because at last we see that he died to bring us forgiveness; rich in resources, because he brings our lives under his gracious dominion, rules in our hearts and fills our lives with his blessing.

Only one further question remains to be answered. How can these riches become ours? The answer the New Testament gives is always the same. It consists of two elements::

(i) *Believe on Jesus Christ, God's Son, the only Saviour.* What does that mean? Trust his promises:

> *Come to me, all you who are weary and burdened,*
> *and I will give you rest. Take my yoke upon you*
> *and learn from me, for I am gentle and humble*
> *in heart, and you will find rest for your souls.*
> *For my yoke is easy and my burden is light.*
>
> *I tell you the truth, whoever hears my word and*
> *believes him who sent me has eternal life and*
> *will not be condemned;*
> *he has crossed over from death to life.*
>
> *Jesus declared, 'I am the bread of life. He who*
> *comes to me will never go hungry, and he who*
> *believes in me will never be thirsty [he is*
> *speaking of spiritual hunger and thirst] . . .*
> *whoever comes to me I will never drive away.*[1]

Entrust yourself to Jesus Christ, God's Son. He is able to save you; trust him, and he will be your Saviour.

[1] Matt.11:28–30; John 5:24; 6:35–37

(ii) *With Christ's help, give up and turn away from your old lifestyle to a new way of life under his authority.*

That is what Jesus means when he calls us to 'repent'. The word used most frequently in the New Testament means to change your mind or purpose.[1] There is more to repentance than feeling sorry for your sin (or, merely feeling sorry for yourself); it means a reversal of the old ways, making amends and restoration where you can.

Repentance means realising that the old way of life is empty;[2] only the new way of following Christ will bring fulness of life.[3]

There is divine wisdom even here. Christ calls us to believe in him and to turn away from sin in every shape and form, in thought and deed. These are things we must do. There is no salvation apart from them. And yet neither our repentance nor our faith contributes anything to the salvation we receive. Salvation is a gift; and the repentance and faith through which we receive it are also gifts;[4] they are the effects of God's work within us.

Faith involves coming to Christ in our sinfulness and emptiness and receiving his forgiveness and fulness. And repentance, the desire to turn from our sin, is born in our hearts only when we come to realise that in coming to Christ we will receive mercy and forgiveness. He will accept us as we are, in our sinfulness; but then he will take us and change us by his grace and power.

Here, then, is God's wisdom. It is stored up in Christ; it is discovered only by those who respond to his summons to repent of sin and believe in him.

Have you found this wisdom? If so you must have come to the point of praying:

[1] The Greek verb is *metanoeo*

[2] See 1 Pet.1:18 [3] See John 10:10

[4] See Ephesians 2:8-10; 6:23; Philippians 1:29 and Acts 11:18

Lord Jesus Christ, I am so foolish,
give me your wisdom to see and follow your truth;

Lord Jesus Christ, I am full of guilt and have no
peace. But you have died to bring forgiveness
and the assurance of pardon;
I trust you to be my Saviour, and by your grace I
turn away from my sin.

Lord Jesus Christ, I am weak and ruled by sin,
give me your power and rule in my heart
and over my whole life.

Have you ever prayed like that?

4: The Conclusion of the Matter

Taste and see that the Lord is good . . .
those who fear him lack nothing.

KING DAVID

4

A punch-line should be memorable – a cleverly-crafted sentence, a surprising statement or a familiar thought in an unexpected context – something to get the reader to think.

The Pundit's chronicles end with a surprising punch-line – at least, to modern ears.

Now all has been heard;
here is the conclusion of the matter:
Fear God and keep his commandments,
for this is the whole of man.[1]

A statement like that from the Old Testament is neither what we want to nor expect to hear. The fear of God is a very unpopular idea. But no one can deny that the punch-line acts like a sharp spur! Interestingly it is prefaced by some words which almost prepare us for the unexpected:

The words of the wise are like goads,
their collected sayings like firmly embedded nails
– given by one Shepherd.[2]

A goad is a sharply pointed stick, often with an iron tip, used to prick an animal to drive it on. This statement is exactly that: it makes us sit up; it may even annoy us.

[1] Eccl.12:13 [2] Eccl.12:11

Does it irritate you, or even anger you, to be told that unless you fear God you have missed the secret of life? But if that is true, this 'goad' has had its intended effect; it has made you say 'ouch!'. It is also like a firmly embedded nail. It is hard to rid the memory of this saying: 'Fear God and keep his commandments, for this is the whole of man'.

The conclusion is not the only goad in the Pundit's comments. The entire chronicle of his experience is full of such irritants – like a handful of dust thrown into our eyes. He hints here and there that he is no longer the man he writes about. But the cool analytical cynicism of many things he says also seems to have been calculated to irritate us. He is 'no more Mr Nice Guy'. There are no words of encouragement, only a cruel exposure of the emptiness of life and counsels to enjoy what we can, because it will not last. 'You want to have "life under the sun"?' he says; 'Here it is; have it!'

Life is sick; we are sick. This is the Pundit's message. You need an emetic. Painful and embarrassing though it may be, you need to vomit out of your soul everything that is destroying your life and will eventually lead you to an endless emptiness.

The fear of God is the medicine you need.

It is hard for us to accept this. One of the old writers once said that 'the fear of God is a left-handed grace'. We may be inclined to think of it more as a slap on the face. The idea of fearing God is part of Old Testament (not to say out-moded) religion, surely? Even if we ourselves make no claim to be committed Christians, we at least know that the fear of God is an Old Testament, not a Christian, way of thinking.

But think for a minute. Who said this?

Do not be afraid of those who can kill the body
and after that can do no more. But I will show
you whom you should fear: Fear him who, after

the killing of the body, has power to throw you
into hell.
Yes, I tell you, fear him.[1]

It was, of course, Jesus. And have you never sung *Amazing Grace*?

'Twas grace that taught my heart *to fear*
And grace my fears relieved.
How precious did that grace appear
The hour I first believed.

Here is a fear which can deliver us from all other fears. It is a powerful divine immunisation which builds up resistance in our hearts enabling us to reject and overcome the anxieties which plague our lives and destroy our peace.

But what is this fear? And how does it make such a difference?

THE FEAR OF GOD

The fear of God is not terror. Terror of God is the reaction of guilt in the face of his holy power. It desires only to run from him in despair.

The Pundit certainly had an awareness of that holy power which devastates everything hostile to it; but he had discovered something more. God's holy power destroys only whatever mars what he loves. But he will withstand and eventually destroy everything that opposes the purposes of that love.

Through every aspect of his character God means to show us his glory. This he loves to do more than anything else. Moreover, he loves his people so much that he will let nothing stand in the way of them coming to share in this glory.

The person who sees this learns what it means to fear God. It means to be filled with a sense of breathtaking awe at his character. It means to realise with shame that although

[1] Luke 12:4–5

we have been made to live as his image, we have forfeited by our sin our privileges and our destiny. It means also that we have begun to realise the costly way in which he restores that glory to us.

The Negro spiritual *Were you there when they crucified my Lord?* captures it well:

> Sometimes it causes me to tremble, tremble, tremble;
> Were you there when they crucified my Lord?

The fear of God in some ways defies our attempts at definition, because it is really another way of saying 'knowing God'. It is a heart-felt love for him because of who he is and what he has done; a sense of being in his majestic presence. It is a thrilling awareness that we have this greatest of all privileges, mingled with a realisation that now the only thing that really matters is his opinion. To have the assurance of his smile is everything; to feel that he frowns on what we do is desolation. To fear God is to be sensitive to both his greatness and his graciousness. It is to know him and to love him wholeheartedly and unreservedly.

To fear God, to trust God, to love God, and to know God – these are really one and the same thing. In fact, the fear of God about which the Pundit speaks arises from the discovery of God's love for us in our sin and weakness. It is the sense of awe that results from the discovery that he knows me through and through, means to destroy all that is sinful in me, and yet does so because he loves me with an intensely faithful love. That stretches my mind and emotions to their limit.

At least, this is how fear is seen in the Bible. It is those who fear the Lord who say 'His love endures for ever'; it is only those who confess their sinfulness who discover that 'With you there is forgiveness; therefore you are feared'.[1]

[1] Psalm 118:4; 130:4

Often the poetic spirit captures this best:

O how I fear Thee, living God
  With deepest, tenderest fears,
And worship Thee, with trembling hope
  And penitential tears.[1]

Or in the striking words of the same writer:

They love Thee little if at all
  Who do not fear thee much
If love is thine attraction, Lord,
  Fear is thy very touch.

This is what Christians call 'filial fear'. It is different from 'servile fear', the terror of the slave who knows that his every wrong move will bring punishment. 'Filial fear' is the reverential love which a child has for his or her father. Thus the first question we ask about everything we do is, 'Will Father approve?'. But filial fear also knows that he accepts whatever we do out of love for him, however falteringly – just as a father lovingly accepts his child's scribbled drawing of him as though it had been done by a Rembrandt. Thus, paradoxically, the child who truly fears his or her father gains greatest joy and pleasure in his presence, and knows great security. Here again is how F. W. Faber saw it:

Oh, Thou art greatly to be feared,
  Thou art so prompt to bless!
The dread to miss such love as Thine
  Makes fear but love's excess.

If this 'filial fear' is the fear of God about which the Pundit enthuses, certain questions press themselves on our attention. Why did he – and why do we – fear it? What effect does it have? How can we come to experience it?

[1] F. W. Faber (1814–63) in 'My God, how wonderful Thou art'

The answer to the first question is this: we try to evade the fear of God because we want to make man great and God small. So long as the Pundit wanted to make 'man the measure of all things', he had to try to reduce God to manageable (and therefore non-fear-able) proportions. That is why the Pundit looked at things only 'under the sun'; to look beyond the sun would be to think about the presence of God and to be brought, inevitably, to fear him.

Martin Luther put it well when he said to the Renaissance humanist Desiderius Erasmus (1469–1536), 'Your God is too man-like'. Luther's great watchword, by contrast, was 'Let God be God!'. If we do not fear God, he believed, we do not really know God. For to know God is to be stunned by his presence. Then we learn that the fear of the Lord is the beginning of all true wisdom.[1]

THE EFFECTS

How is it that to fear God is 'the whole of man' as the Pundit says? Because it brings meaning, purpose and significance to a life which otherwise is ultimately brief, empty and meaningless.

We have followed the Pundit's attempts to find satisfaction that would last: in the pursuit of knowledge, of pleasure, of work, of success. How does the fear of God make a difference?

True Knowledge

When we look at life 'under the sun', excluding God, something happens to our understanding and our learning. We try to explain the world without reference to the essential explanatory factor: God's creating activity and his sustaining presence. The result? An endless pursuit of learning which can never bring a knowledge that satisfies:

[1] Psa. 111:10; Proverbs 9:10

> *Of making many books there is no end,*
> *and much study wearies the body.*[1]

There is what Paul calls a 'futility' in our 'thinking'.[2] But the fear of God reverses this, placing him at the centre of our universe. He *is* at the centre of life. We see everything in the light of his creating and sustaining activity. Then things begin to make sense: 'The secret of the Lord is with them that fear him.'[3]

Without him, life is at best a puzzle, at worst a tragedy; this is not a self-contained 'user-friendly' universe. With him we learn that even when his immediate purposes are hidden from us his ways are perfect (for we do not always, nor do we ever fully, understand his plans). We also learn this: even though we will never know everything about this world, we do know something about everything: God is its Creator, and he is our heavenly Father.

That is why, even when he adopts a cynical posture, the renewed Pundit cannot expose 'life under the sun' in its naked emptiness without planting seeds of wisdom, and giving us illumination to help us find our way to the truth. He urges younger people:

> *Remember your Creator in the days of your youth,*
> *before the days of trouble come and the years approach when you will say, 'I find no pleasure in them'.*[4]

The person who fears God, who lives in his presence, who knows that the world is his handiwork, sings:

> Heaven above is softer blue,
> Earth around is sweeter green;
> Something lives in every hue
> Christless eyes have never seen:

[1] Eccl. 12:12 [2] Eph. 4:17 [3] Psa. 25:14 (A.V.) [4] Eccl. 12:1

Birds with gladder songs o'erflow,
Flowers with deeper beauties shine,
Since I know, as now I know,
I am his and he is mine.[1]

The supreme irony of the God-rejecting life is that the creation is full of beauty and mystery which makes every instinct in us want to express praise – but such a person has already argued that there is no one there to praise! It is also, in its fallen condition, full of pain and grief, suffering and tragedy – but the unbeliever has again argued that there is no one there to hear our instinctive cries for help.

Our instincts to shout out to Someone Else in praise and to call out to Someone Else for help reflect the fact that we were created for fellowship with God. In order to deny him, we have to deny these instincts and reinterpret our experience. But from this self-deception the fear of the Lord delivers us.

But there is another aspect to this true learning. The fear of the Lord is not only the secret of true knowledge, it is also the beginning of wisdom. With it we learn that we cannot understand everything, nor can we change everything.

Wisdom, like an inheritance, is a good thing
and benefits those who see the sun.
Wisdom is a shelter . . .
But the advantage of knowledge is this:
that wisdom preserves the life of its possessor.
Consider what God has done:
Who can straighten what he has made crooked?[2]

The essence of sin is our rebellion against God in order to be God ourselves. It is to say with Nietzsche: 'If there is a

[1] George Wade Robinson (1838–77) from 'Loved with everlasting love'
[2] Eccl. 7:11–13

God, how can I bear not to be that God?'. Some people can never be at peace when life goes apparently out of control. We try to work everything together for our own good, according to our own plans. The Pundit reminds us:

> *Do not be . . . overwise . . .*
> *why destroy yourself?*[1]

But those who have gained true wisdom learn to leave what they cannot understand in the hands of their Father in heaven. He alone will straighten what is crooked; he alone sees the end from the beginning; he alone is able to work everything together for the good of those who love him, because he has called them according to his purpose to transform them again into his own image. Here is where we rest our minds and hearts:

> *He who did not spare his own Son, but gave him up*
> *for us all — how will he not also, along with him,*
> *graciously give us all things?*[2]

Lasting Pleasures

Those who pursue pleasure for its own sake and in every conceivable way never find it in any lasting form. If all we seek in life is a 'good time', we are doomed to dissatisfaction. This much the Pundit had discovered from experience.

Why? Because there is nothing in the world big enough to satisfy the desires which are part of our basic human make-up. We have seen how, speaking about God, the Pundit says:

> *He has made everything beautiful in its time.*
> *He has also set eternity in the hearts of men;*
> *yet they cannot fathom what God has done from*
> *beginning to end.*[3]

[1] Eccl. 7:16 [2] Rom. 8:32; see 8:28–32 [3] Eccl. 3:11

If the eternal alone can meet our deepest needs, it is hardly surprising that we are left frustrated and spiritually hungry by the temporal. Turn away from the God who alone can satisfy you and it is inevitable that you will be dissatisfied with lesser and ephemeral pleasures.

The Gospel of John records a wonderfully sensitive story about Jesus. *En route* from Judea to Galilee, he made his way through Samaria – an unusual thing for a Jew since Jews did their best to avoid Samaritans whom they regarded as heretics.

About noon, when his disciples had gone into the town of Sychar to try to buy some food for lunch, Jesus sat down beside the town well. He was tired and he wanted to rest.

But his rest was disturbed by a woman coming from the town to get water from the well. Jesus asked her if she would give him a drink.

A fascinating conversation developed. She was, doubtless, amazed that he even spoke to her. She had several counts against her: she was a Samaritan, he was a Jew; she was a woman, he was a man; and in any case, why would a woman come to the well in the intense heat of the noonday sun, at exactly the time of day when nobody else would be there? Going out to draw water was a social event in Sychar as much as meeting for morning coffee is today. It did not take second sight on Jesus' part to realise that something was wrong. This woman was undoubtedly *persona non grata* in Sychar society.

Yet the conversation began. During it – with enormous grace and sensitivity – Jesus unravelled the truth about the woman's life. Needs from which she had hidden in her search for satisfaction and security now became clear. Jesus gently but firmly broke through all her defence-mechanisms to reveal her long-suppressed need of God. Pointing to the well he said:

> *Everyone who drinks this water will be thirsty again, but whoever drinks the water I give him will never thirst. Indeed, the water I give him will become in him a spring of water welling up to eternal life.*[1]

There and then, in Jesus Christ, the woman found what she had been blindly running from over the years.

> I sighed for rest and happiness,
> I yearned for them, not Thee;
> But while I passed my Saviour by,
> His love laid hold on me.
>
> I tried the broken cisterns Lord,
> But ah! the waters failed,
> Even as I stooped to drink they fled
> And mocked me as I wailed.
>
> *Now none but Christ can satisfy*
> *None other name for me*
> *There's love and life and lasting joy*
> *Lord Jesus, found in Thee.*[2]

> *You will fill me with joy in your presence, with eternal pleasures at your right hand.*[3]

Only lasting things can give us lasting pleasure. Moreover, only those who know that they have been forgiven and therefore enjoy the anticipation of heaven can enjoy this world without the gnawing sense that it is a bubble easily pricked.

In the end, all the pleasures of this age mock us unless we have our need for eternal life satisfied by God, and our thirst quenched by the living water which Christ alone can give us. But take Christ and with him comes all manner of pleasures.

[1] John 4:13-14
[2] Anonymous. See John 4:1–42 for the full story [3] Psa. 16:11

Work Satisfaction

Work alone cannot satisfy us. That is perhaps more obvious now than it has ever been. It is insecure, often frustrating, and much of it seems pointless to those who engage in it; they do not work for its own sake and for the satisfaction it brings; they do it only for the money. Thus comments the Pundit:

> *So I hated life, because the work that is done under*
> *the sun was grievous to me.*
> *All of it is meaningless, a chasing after the wind.*[1]

What difference does the fear of God make? It transforms everything we do, no matter how mundane, no matter how grand. How? Because it invests all work with the higher dimension of honouring God, seeking his glory, reflecting his character as the Original Worker in everything we do. Other things may have their place: profit, expansion, industrial relations. But these can fail the individual. Moreover there is nothing inherently uplifting about working on a production line, or making something of ephemeral character. But the man or woman who has learned a child-like fear of the Heavenly Father does everything for him. That injects a sense of higher purpose, a quality of workmanship that nothing else can. This is how George Herbert (1593–1633) put it in his poem *The Elixir*:

> Teach me my God and King,
> In all things thee to see;
> And what I do in anything,
> To do it as for thee!
>
> A man that looks on glass,
> On it may stay his eye;
> Or if he pleaseth, through it pass,
> And then the heaven espy.

[1] Eccl. 2:17

All may of thee partake;
Nothing can be so mean,
Which with this tincture, 'for thy sake',
Will not grow bright and clean.

A servant with this clause
Makes drudgery divine:
Who sweeps a room, as for thy laws,
Makes that and the action fine.

This is the famous stone
That turneth all to gold
For that which God doth touch and own
Cannot for less be told.

Real Success

'The fear of the Lord is pure',[1] wrote King David. He meant that it produces a 'radiance' in our lives. It is health-giving and wholesome. It produces a sharp, clean, integrated life. In a word it lends a true dignity to our character, whatever our personal, social or financial circumstances may be.

The fear of God gives men and women and young people courage to oppose what is wrong and do what is right, whatever the consequences. They have this promise: 'Fear the Lord . . . for those who fear him lack nothing.'[2] To live thus in the presence of God, 'before his face' as the Old Testament picturesquely puts it, delivers us from relativism, for 'to fear the Lord is to hate evil'.[3] It makes ordinary men and women into moral kings and queens, like the Jewish midwives in bondage in Egypt who chose to obey God rather than men: they 'feared God and [therefore] did not do what the king of Egypt had told them to do [i.e. to kill male infants].'[4]

Here is dignity and strength of character of an enviable kind.

[1] Psa. 19:9 [2] Psa. 34:9 [3] Prov. 8:13 [4] Exodus 1:17

But how can the child-like, loving fear of the Lord be born and grow within us?

THE BEGINNING

Filial fear is a characteristic only of those who have a filial relationship. You will never fear God until you know yourself to be his child. Frightened of him you may be, for many reasons, not always good ones; but fear him with a loving and intimate reverence you never can.

It is, first of all, essential that, like the Pundit, you see the truth about yourself and about your life: left to yourself, it will be meaningless and empty. The reason? You have lost all spiritual life. You have no energy for God. More, you have sinned against him and are actually under his judgement. The frustrations you experience are not a matter of 'bad things' happening to a 'good' person. They are the result of your waywardness from God.

No one ever came to fear God without first feeling unmasked. Penitent faith involves seeing the truth staring me in the face: my sins are not out-of-character actions. They are not *aberrations*; they are *revelations* of the truth about my twisted, God-less heart. Sinner is what I am, by nature, thought, choice and deed. 'God, have mercy on me, a sinner'[1] is what I need to learn to pray.

We have already seen that there is only one place in which the mercy we need can be found: in Jesus Christ. He came into the world to bear the guilt of our sin under the judgement of God. This is the real meaning of the cross. He died our death to become our Saviour. Having done so he rose again in triumph and now lives to be our Lord.

> *God made him [Christ] who had no sin to be sin for us, so that in him we might become the righteousness of God.*[2]

[1] Luke 18:13 [2] 2 Cor 5:21

> *He died for all, that those who live should no longer live for themselves but for him who died for them and was raised again.*[1]

But how can you be brought into the family of God through this work of Christ? Paul, again, gives us the answer:

> *You are all sons of God through faith in Christ Jesus . . . Because you are sons, God sent the Spirit of his Son into our hearts, the Spirit who calls out, 'Abba, Father.'*
> *So you are no longer a slave, but a son; and since you are a son, God has made you also an heir.*[2]

The way God brings us to experience filial fear for himself is by bringing us into his family. He does this by his Spirit, in an act so sovereign and powerful that the New Testament calls it a new creation, a new birth, a spiritual resurrection. The Spirit of Christ then begins to create in us the tender, sensitive spirit which the Lord Jesus displayed during his ministry.

Isaiah wrote of the coming Saviour that the 'Spirit of wisdom . . . the Spirit of knowledge *and of the fear of the Lord*' would be on his life, so that he would 'delight in the fear of the Lord'.[3] When Luke later records that Jesus grew in wisdom, he implies that he too grew in the 'fear of the Lord' which is 'the beginning of wisdom'.[4]

The most important principle in Jesus' life was the approval of his Father in everything he did. For him, the fear of God was not a pathological morbidity, but an expression of his love for and his trust in his Heavenly Father. He knew, with David, that: 'The Lord confides in those who fear

[1] 2 Cor. 5:15 [2] Galatians 3:26; 4:6–7 [3] Isa. 11:2–3
[4] Prov. 9:10, see Luke 2:52

him' and so he lived by this principle: 'My eyes are ever on the Lord'.[1] So it will be for us too, when we are born into his family through the Spirit.

Growing in the Fear of God

If the wisdom and knowledge of God has already become part of our life, a further question needs to be answered here. How can we grow in the fear of the Lord? Here are the biblical counsels we need to follow:

1. *Use the helps God has given*: worship with the family of God, prayer, the exposition of Scripture, the ongoing disciplines of a fellowship of God's people, the physical signs he gives – baptism and the Lord's Supper – to mark you out as his and to encourage you in faith.

How do these help us? They keep our eyes fixed on God's glory. In our worship, he is praised and admired. He speaks to us, sometimes with great power, through preaching. He humbles us by using someone like ourselves to expound and apply his word to us. But because it is *his* word, brought into our minds and hearts by his Spirit (and not merely by the preacher), we find our lives opened more and more to his revelation, and stimulated to bow our wills before him.

So we will begin to learn to love these different ways in which God brings to our spirits a new sense of his majesty, glory and grace. We will thus learn to wait on God, to listen to preaching which exalts God and humbles us, and to praise him for all he is.

In addition, we will experience deep and satisfying, yet solemn joy when we remember the meaning of our baptism.[2] Then, when we take the bread and wine in the Lord's Supper we will find ourselves full of a tender-hearted reverence for the Lamb who was slain for our sins. We will

[1] Psa. 25:14–15 [2] See Rom. 6:4

catch a glimpse of his glory and learn to fear him with joy.[1]

2. *Value the friendship and fellowship of others who fear the Lord.* There is a beautiful description of this in the Old Testament. In a time of spiritual decline,

> *Those who feared the Lord talked with each other,*
> *and the Lord listened and heard.*
> *A scroll of remembrance was written in his*
> *presence concerning those who feared the Lord*
> *and honoured his name.*[2]

The implication should be clear enough. The Lord does not want us to fear him as isolated individuals. We are not on our own as Christians, even though there are times when we will be alone. The encouragement of others and their example helps us to appreciate what a beautiful thing the fear of the Lord really is.

3. *Reflect on the providence of God in life.* Think of all that he has done to bring you to this day. Think of the different ways in which he has awakened genuine spiritual concerns in you. Think of the amazing way in which he has promised to work everything together for the good of those who love him.[3]

Think too of how you have sometimes made decisions without ever imagining how the Lord would overrule all the details of your life for his own purposes. His plans and thoughts are far above yours, and yet you have seen them work out in all kinds of amazing ways.[4] He has shaped all of history in order to bring to pass his will in your life. See this and you will be able to say with new meaning 'He has done everything well!'.[5]

[1] 1 Cor. 10:14–22 [2] Malachi 3:16 [3] Rom. 8:28–29
[4] See Isa. 55:8–9 [5] Mark 7:37

4. *Learn to live in the shadow of the cross of Christ.* Someone else's love for us can make us feel small and humble as well as fill us with joy. Such love is only a reflection of the love which was displayed at the cross. There God demonstrated his love to us in that while we were powerless, ungodly, sinners Christ died for us.[1] Surely this makes us say, with Micah,

> *Who is a God like you, who pardons sins and forgives . . .?*[2]

Here is a deep awe and fear of the Lord; but here, too, is the joy of forgiveness. At the cross of Christ both faith and fear begin and grow. In its shadow we learn to sing the new song of the redeemed:

> *Great and marvellous are your deeds,*
> *Lord God Almighty.*
> *Just and true are your ways,*
> *King of the ages,*
> *Who will not fear you, O Lord,*
> *and bring glory to your name?*[3]

This is the true wisdom, joy and purpose in life for which the Pundit had longed. He wrote the chronicles of his folly to stimulate others to search for what he eventually discovered: the truth. It can be found only in Jesus Christ; it is received only through faith; it is enjoyed only in the hearts of those who have learned by grace to love and fear the Lord.

Have you found him yet?

[1] Rom. 5:6 [2] Micah 7:18 [3] Rev. 15:3–4